The Ordinary Shaman

Are You Curious About Shamanism and Want to Know How It Works?

If you picked up this book you are a seeker who wants to be equipped to meet the challenges of the day and enhance your life tools.

In this convenient Itty Bitty Book, Christine Alisa guides you through skills that are attainable by anyone. This book is a beginners course on Shamanism; a down to earth manual that will apply to your life in unexpected ways.

Through 15 steps you will:

- get to know what Shamanism is all about,
- learn to connect with your spirit guides for all kinds of practical everyday uses, and
- open yourself to an age-old tradition that is applicable for today's perplexities.

Tap into this easy-to-use practice by picking up a copy of this valuable little book and open yourself to new possibilities today.

Enjoy!

Your Amazing Itty Bitty® The Ordinary Shaman

15 Simple Steps to Bring Shamanism Into Your Life

Christine Alisa

Published by Itty Bitty® Publishing
A subsidiary of S & P Productions, Inc.

Copyright © 2019 **Christine Alisa, M.S., MFT, Shamanic Practitioner**

All rights reserved. No part of this book may be reproduced or transmitted in any form or by any means, electronic or mechanical, including photocopying, recording or by any information storage and retrieval system, without written permission of the publisher, except for inclusion of brief quotations in a review.

Printed in the United States of America

www.ittybittypublishing.com
Itty Bitty Publishing
311 Main Street, Suite D
El Segundo, CA 90245
(310) 640-8885

ISBN: 978-1-950326-31-0

Dedication Page

I dedicate this book to all those who have touched my life on my Shamanic path whether they be practitioners, clients or participants in my workshops, meet-ups and trainings. I am very grateful to have been able to witness profound healing journeys, deep desires to learn, courageous spirits, and open hearts. Above all I am grateful to my power animal, the many animal spirits that have given me direction, protection and wisdom, my ancestors, guides and teachers.

Stop by our Itty Bitty® website Directory to find more interesting information from our experts.

www.IttyBittyPublishing.com

Or visit Chris Alisa at:

www.christinealisa.com

TABLE OF CONTENTS

Introduction

What is it?
- Step 1. What Is Shamanism?
- Step 2. The Origin Of Shamanism
- Step 3. What Does A Shaman Or Shamanic Practitioner Do?

How Do You Use It?
- Step 4. What Are Power Animals And Totems?
- Step 5. What Is Journeying?
- Step 6. Listen To Your Heart
- Step 7. What Does Setting An Intention Mean?
- Step 8. Getting Clarity And Developing Trust
- Step 9. What Are The Lower, Middle And Upper Worlds?

How Does It Help?
- Step 10. Practicing Shamanism Creates Joy
- Step 11. Incorporating Ceremony Into Your Life
- Step 12. Hopes And Dreams
- Step 13. How Is Shamanism Practical?
- Step 14. Applications For Everyday Life
- Step 15. Shamanism Seeks The Highest Good

Introduction

Why is there a need for Shamanism today?

Many people have a need to fill the void inside; that empty place theat appears as emotional pain, feeling lost, purposeless, lonely or needing to mask their feelings with addictive substances and behaviors.

Once that desire to connect with something meaniful brims to the surface, then it is time for Shamanism. You can develop a new relationship with a compassionate animal spirit guide.

This beginners guide is for everyone in the modern world. I call it *The Ordinary Shaman* because I want everyone to have access to it in a step-by-step approach achievable for all.

This Itty Bitty Book is not meant to disrespect any indigenous communities around the world, but rather to open the minds of many by approaching Shamanism with simplicity and ease. The ancient memory can rekindle and affect our current times for the highest good.

My purpose is to demystify Shamanism and take it out of the belief system that it is weird and to let you know that you are not alone.

The fifteen chapters are divided into three sections:

1. What is it?
2. How do I use it?
3. How can it help me?

What Is It?
Step 1
What Is Shamanism?

Shamanism is an ancient practice that has been used for 100,000 years and has more relevance in our modern world than ever before. Today it is:

1. A practice of being still, breathing, using a drum or rattle to go into a deeper space; an altered state.
2. A compassionate vehicle that nurtures expands and connects you to the world around you.
3. A revealer of parts of yourself you have as yet uncovered: an inner exploration.
4. A pathway of communication with nature; plants, animals, the wind, stars and beyond that enriches your life.
5. A joining between you and your spirit guides, power animals and other compassionate guides for the purpose of healing and inner exploration.

Shamanism Has Many Definitions Including:

- A dictionary definition is "the religious practices of certain native peoples of Northern Asia." The word shaman, meaning wisdom originated with the Tungus-speaking people of Siberia.
- An ancient tradition conducted by a member of a village or community called a Shaman. The Shaman had many purposes including helping find the right crops for planting in the best area in order to keep the community/village healthy.
- A healing method that brings your soul into alignment and releases negative energy.
- A practice that can be done by yourself or in a group.
- A dialogue with animal spirits asking them to be in relationship with you and guide you through life's challenges.

What is it?
Step 2
The Origin Of Shamanism

Early humans were connected to the Earth, her plants, land, water, air and animals not only for their survival, but also for the deep honor they felt for the abundance the Earth gave them.

1. Shamans were for early humans and the many indigenous cultures of the world a spiritual guide who could travel to what they call non-ordinary reality, a place of deep wisdom to understand the universe and the role humankind had on Earth.
2. Each village or tribe had a shaman much like what we have with our doctors, healers, meteorologists and scientists. That shaman would conduct ceremonies of all kinds including gratitude for their bounty.
3. Early humans believed that animals have a spirit to honor much like the closeness many of us feel towards our pets. They believed that animals and plants sacrificed themselves for the good of the community and should be honored.

Cultures With a Shamanic Tradition Still Practice it Today.

Indigenous peoples carry on the traditions given to them by their ancestors.

- Among the many indigenous tribes and traditions that currently practice Shamanism are: the Hmong people of China, the Tibetan Bon Tradition, Peruvian Shamans performing Ayahuasca ceremonies, Aborigines of Australia, Sami people of Lapland and Norway, Mongolian Shamanism or Tengerism.
- Many Native American tribes and communities do not use the term shaman. They are very clear on the fact that their tribes have holy men and women.
- Native Americans often define the various healing practitioners of their communities as medicine men and women, healers, spiritual leader, elder or herbalist and story tellers to name a few.

What Is it?
Step 3
What Does A Shaman Or Shamanic Practitioner Do?

A shaman usually receives his or her training from a shaman in their indigenous culture of their birth. A shamanic practitioner is a healer who has received advanced training in a type of Shamanism from a qualified shamanic practitioner or shaman. They include:

1. Teaching you how to journey and connect with the spirit world. They often lead drumming circles, rituals, ceremonies and healing sessions.
2. Educating you about power animals and their messages. They aid you in understanding the energies and metaphors seen, sensed or heard from those compassionate spirit guides.
3. Helping you to connect with nature in order to communicate and deepen your relationship with the world around you.
4. Provide healing skills and practices for people, the Earth and its inhabitants.

Healing Skills of a Shaman or Shamanic Practitioner

Here is a list of several healing practices:

- **Soul retrieval** is the process of bringing back a soul part that you may have lost through a traumatic event in the past. The shaman journeys to the time and place of the event to bring back that part for integration. The energies meld with the soul into wholeness supported by the spirit guides.
- **Divination** is the practice of understanding the signs around you and using different tools to enter the spirit world. Such tools include journeying, drumming, rattling and merging in the body with a spirit helper interpreting the symbols received from the guide.
- **Clearing and Extraction** of unwanted negative energies, entities or soul entanglements from you or your environment.

How Do You Use It?
Step 4
What Are Power Animals Or Totems?

Power animals, also called totems, are the spirits of animals that come in the form of wild or domesticated animals, reptiles, insects or birds. Each one of you has your own power animal that is with you at all times in what you might call "the invisible world," the world of the shaman.

1. Have you ever seen an insect, reptile, bird or animal repeatedly appear in your life? Maybe bees come around you often or dragonfly comes right up to you?
2. Do you get subliminal messages in your head and dismiss them immediately? Maybe you sense that danger is ahead and you find yourself instinctively turning in another direction narrowly escaping an accident.
3. These are the messages maybe communicated from your power animal. These compassionate animal spirits may appear in physical form, as pictures in your mind or words you hear all for the purpose of guiding you on your journey here on Earth

What can you do to connect with your Power Animal?

Here are some ways that you can communicate with your power animal:

- Trust yourself and believe you are not crazy or weird if you see, feel, sense or hear an animal communicating with you. That animal maybe your totem or it may just want to communicate something to you.
- Discover who your power animal is by clicking this link: https://www.christinealisa.com/my-books/the-ordinary-shaman/
- Once you know your totem, there are various sites where you can find their characteristics. Here is a list of books I recommend: Go to: https://www.christinealisa.com/my-books/the-ordinary-shaman/You can also determine this for yourself by asking.
- Your power animal will give you messages that may come in many forms. You receive these messages through journeying with them, which guides you to develop that relationship.
- Open up your mind to the real possibility that you can nurture the relationship.

How Do You Use It?
Step 5
What Is Journeying?

Journeying is an experience in an altered state of consciousness where you 'travel' to non-ordinary reality with your spirit guide. You begin by:

1. Setting up a type of ceremony where you light a candle, burn sage, make an intention (See Step 7), and use a drum, rattle or recorded drumming to connect with your guides. The rhythmic sound of drumming puts you into a deeper, altered state of consciousness.
2. You use your senses like vision, hearing and, what I call sensing. If you are more visual you may see a vision, if you are auditory, you hear words and if you are kinesthetic, you sense something.
3. You call upon your power animal to meet you in what is called non-ordinary reality; that is, the spirit world or parallel universe.

A Guide to Journeying

Follow these suggestions to begin your journeying experience:

- Find a quiet place where you will not be disturbed.
- Turn the lights down and put on an eye cover or scarf over your eyes to help block out everything else.
- Use your own drum, rattle or put on a recorded drumming CD or YouTube channel and listen to the vibration.
- Take three deep breaths and then find a comfortable rhythm to your breath.
- Imagine tree roots growing down into the Earth. Visualize yourself traveling down these roots to meet your power animal.
- Ask, "Power animal please meet me."
- Set an intention to receive a message from your power animal, listen and wait for pictures or sensations.
- Power animals often speak in metaphors.
- If you are unclear about the message, just ask for clarification. i.e. "What do you mean?" "Can you clarify that for me?"
- See my link for my introduction to journeying to help you. https://www.christinealisa.com/my-books/the-ordinary-shaman/

How Do You Use It?
Step 6
Listen To Your Heart

Pay attention to what your heart is experiencing such as any desire, injury, grief or pain. Your compassionate spirit guides are always with you to help you with these feelings.

1. Listening to your heart is different from being caught in the pain. In Shamanism it is the heart that holds the intention of what you want to change in your life.
2. When you decide to find a healing path through the difficulties in your life you are listening to your inner self.
3. Take these messages your heart is telling you and communicate them to your power animal. Ask your power animal for guidance through your challenges.
4. Practicing this with your compassionate spirit guide will awaken you to new possibilities and give you new direction.
5. It is as if your pain is actually the doorway to transforming your life.

Heart Messages

- Find a quiet place and time with no distractions for at least 20 minutes.
- Sit on a chair with your feet on the floor or lie down.
- Take three deep cleansing breaths and then breathe normally.
- Open up your heart chakra: https://www.christinealisa.com/my-books/the-ordinary-shaman
- Ask what your heart needs and notice any emotions. Listen to the first thing that pops up in your mind.
- Maybe you have a dream of what you want to create in your life.
- Maybe you want to change a relationship, a job, a career, or something you want to let go of.
- Maybe you want help getting out of a bad situation.
- Use what comes up for your intention in your journeying experience to your power animal.
- Remember they speak through your senses, visual, auditory and kinesthetic and with the use of metaphors.

How Do You Use it?
Step 7
What Does Setting An Intention Mean?

An intention is a goal statement about what you want to change, uplift, enhance or modify in your life with the help of your spirit guide. Setting an intention means you formulate in your mind what you want to accomplish in the journey.

1. Your first intention could be, "I want to meet my power animal."
2. After you meet with your power animal and it takes you on a journey, your later intentions would be, "What message do you have for me today?"
3. In the beginning you are developing a relationship with your power animal and he/she is the one who will provide you with the experience that he/she feels you need.
4. Your intentions will develop when you go deep inside yourself and notice what you desire and what you want to change.

Intentions Develop over Time

You may have specific areas in your life you want to improve or accomplish as you develop your journeying experience. This is a time to set an intention that is specific to your needs or desires. Some examples might be:

- "My intention is to learn how to not take on other peoples negative energy."
- "My intention is to clear some room in my life so I can have some quiet time."
- "My intention is to get some clarity about a certain relationship in my life."
- "My intention is to let go of this pain I feel about my past."

Be gentle with yourself and stay away from self-judgment. Once you set an intention you can ask your power animal for direction and guidance.

- "Power animal, will you help me not take on negative energy? Will you help me discern the people who are best for me to be around?"
- "Power animal, what steps can I make to let go of old pain?"
- "Power animal, will you guide me to improve my relationships?"
- "Power animal, what can I do to take better care of myself?"

How Do You Use It?
Step 8
Getting Clarity and Developing Trust

When you first learn to communicate with your compassionate spirit guides you will find they often show you pictures or metaphors that may seem unclear. It maybe confusing and you don't trust what you perceive. Learning to ask questions of your guides and develop trust in the answers they give you is important.

1. Do not be afraid to ask questions during your journey if you do not understand what they are showing you. "What do you mean by what you showed me?"
2. You are building trust that the messages your guides are giving you are for your highest good as you practice journeying.
3. If the messages start to make sense and apply to your life, trust them. Notice if you get similar messages that build and continue to give you direction that fits.
4. Trust is an integral part of being able to receive the messages and put them into practice in your life even if you do not always understand their meaning.
5. With time a message from your power animal will make more sense to you.

Developing a trusting relationship with your guides.

There are elements in life that challenge your ability to trust. Those experiences can affect your relationship with your guides. Looking at how you trust in your life is useful when beginning this shamanic work.

- Take a look at how much you trust yourself. Do you question or doubt yourself?
- Are there any beliefs you have picked up that block you from trusting?
- Some people have had very traumatic experiences that keep them from trusting people. Have you had one?
- Your power animal and other spirit guides are very loving, understanding and can help you repair that trust inside of you. Asking for their help opens the trust.
- Building trust that what you are hearing, seeing and experiencing in your journeys is real and true may take time. It is a process.
- Give it time and watch for subtle signs in your life that validate those messages.

How Do You Use It?
Step 9
What Are The Lower, Middle And Upper Worlds?

You connect with your spirit guides in three different worlds or realms in what is called non-ordinary reality. These worlds are called the lower, middle and upper worlds.

Lower World
1. It can look and feel much like a Hobbit world with roots and plants and earth.
2. It is typically where you meet your power animals by imagining that you are traveling down through roots.
3. It is where the elementals reside such as fairies, elves, leprechauns, dwarfs, goblins, and trolls.

Middle World
1. It is the place where you meet and communicate with the spirits of plants, trees, animals, lakes, oceans, the wind; basically the natural world around you.
2. When a butterfly sits on a leaf near you, take the time to ask if it will speak to you. Then listen.

Upper World and Journey Suggestions.

Upper World

Is the realm where you meet your teachers who come from various traditions or religions, archangels and Ascended Masters.

- These teachers may have lived on Earth at one time and were great teachers. Now they choose to pass on their wisdom from the Upper World.
- Some examples of these teachers are Kwan Yin, Ganesh, St. Germaine, Isis, Mary Magdalene, Gautama Buddha and Jesus to name a few.
- They include the Archangels like Michael, Metatron, Ariel and Gabriel.

Journey Suggestions:

- See yourself traveling down the roots of a tree to meet your power animal in the **Lower World.**
- Be in nature and call upon the spirits around you to give you a message in the **Middle World.**
- See yourself climbing a mountain, a rainbow or a rope or connect with the wind to take you to the **Upper Word.**

How Does It Help?
Step 10
Practicing Shamanism Creates Joy

Your guides teach what magnificent beings you are and the capabilities you store inside. They give you hope, revelations about the world and its immense beauty and significance. You learn about the infinite nature of the Universe and the soaring lives you can live given your desire to take that step.

1. Many lead a life of narrow vision. They rarely step into the peripheral expanses around them.
2. When you spend so much time speeding through the immediacy of each element of your life, you miss the splendor that enlivens your life.
3. As you introduce the practices of journeying, attending to nature, sitting in the quiet of reflections, dancing to the tune of your inner joy you see a wider view, beyond the daily grind.
4. You may have stopped remembering who you really are, who you came here to experience and what you wanted to accomplish. The practice of Shamanism stirs those rumblings inside you

Shamanism Helps Relieve Internal Pain

Society's values often conflict with creating a life of calm and acceptance. Chaos in the world seeps into the individual's daily life and relationships are in constant flux.

Various examples are:

- Some people are highly sensitive, intuitive empaths who struggle with the negative energies around them.
- Others lead lives of addiction disconnected from their Higher Power and spiritual selves.
- A segment of society is wrapped up in the daily financial or health struggle that paralyzes them with fear and resentment.
- Others may be depressed or anxious.

If you are experiencing any of these issues working with a Shaman or Shamanic Practitioner can provide healing techniques for your mind, body and soul. It is a healing practice you can use in conjunction with psychotherapy and other modalities depending on the severity. There are also shamanic groups that guide you with your journeying experience.

How Does It Help?
Step 11
Incorporating Ceremony Into Your Life

All cultures have rituals and ceremonies that bring meaning to life. Here are some simple acts of ceremony that can enrich your daily life.

1. Let go of an old unhealthy relationship by selecting a rock to represent that relationship. Find a place in nature such as an ocean or mountain and throw it with the intention of letting go.
2. Write down a behavior or thought you want to release and burn the paper in a BBQ, fireplace or safe place. See it go up in smoke.
3. Sing or whistle after releasing something unwanted as an act of joy and renewal.
4. Honor your blessings by lighting a candle to represent them. Speak them aloud and feel the shift inside you.
5. Give a small meaningful gift to someone in appreciation of what they have done for you or just because.
6. Join a group shamanic ceremony.

Examples of simple ceremonies

Here are some suggestions for you to stimulate your own creative ceremonies.

- Create a special shelf, table or area in your home where you can place items that are meaningful to you.
- Gather mementos, bits from nature such as a feather, shell, twig, rock or flower and put them in your place of honor.
- Write your intentions of what you wish to change or goals you have set. Place the note under a special crystal or rock with a candle on your sacred altar.
- Sit by an ocean, pond, river, waterfall or fountain and listen to the water, which is an energy enhancer. Listen to any messages you hear from the water spirits.
- Ceremonies can be as simple as smiling at a passing stranger and thinking good thoughts about them.
- Plant a flower or herb in remembrance of someone you loved. Everyone is enriched by the customs that bring us closer to our hearts.
- Celebrate your accomplishments, the letting go of what no longer serves you and lessons you have learned. Create a celebration that is meaningful to you.

How Does It Help?
Step 12
Hopes and Dreams

What are your hopes and dreams? Do you have deep ones that you never share with anyone? Is there a part of you that really wants those visions and wishes to come true?

1. Sit down and write your personal dreams, aspirations and visions. Your power animal wants to hear you express them so they can help design them with you.
2. If you cannot define what your dreams are, travel back in time to your childhood. What did you create, wish or imagine that you have forgotten?
3. Journey to your power animal by asking, "Will you help me bring about my hopes and dreams?" Then they can enhance and heighten the vibration of those wishes, visions and dreams.
4. Co-create with your power animal to reach a higher level of consciousness. Then your dreams may evolve into something even greater than you ever thought possible.

How to Connect Your Hopes and Dreams with your Animal Spirits:

Here is a guideline you can use:

- Write down your hopes and dreams intentions on a piece of paper.
- Put them in a place of honor, maybe on a shelf or table making an altar.
- Add these elements: a candle representing fire, a favorite crystal or bowl of soil representing Earth, a feather representing air, a bowl of water representing water and a flower, plant or seed in the soil representing growth.
- Journey to your power animal and ask, "Will you guide me on how I can achieve my hopes and dreams in my life?"
- Maybe they will give you steps to follow or you can ask what steps to take.
- Write down what they tell you, what they show you or what you sense.
- Remember they will guide you their way, which is always meant for your highest good.
- Offer up in a ceremony your hopes, visions and dreams for the highest good of all.

How Does It Help?
Step 13
How is Shamanism Practical?

Your compassionate spirit guides want to help you solve the simplest tasks of life to the more serious decisions you need to make. Here are some suggestions of practical ideas:

1. If you cannot find your keys, get quiet, breathe and ask your power animal to direct you to where you left them. Listen, sense or see where you are directed.
2. When you are driving and you get a sense (like a nudge) that the road you are taking or turn you are making seems like not a good idea. Change your course. You might find out later that there was some danger or an accident on that road.
3. If you are stumped on how to fix something around the house call on your power animal to give you directions. You might be surprised how an answer might pop in your mind.
4. If you are going to a special event and you want help on what to wear ask your power animal point it out to you.

Other Practical Ideas

When you connect more with your power animal through asking for every day solutions, the relationship gets stronger. Try some of these ideas.

- When you see a homeless person or someone in some distress, ask their guides to watch over them. It will enable you to fee less helpless and more empowered.
- Ask your power animal to work on a project with you, maybe writing, designing something at work, decorating a room or doing an assignment for a class.
- If you, yourself or someone you know is in distress, ask their guides to give direction and resolution to the problem.
- If you are making a presentation or speech or communicating with your loved one ask your guides to be with you throughout. Listen to words that come through to you. The words may have not originally planned. They may be better.

You will discover that Shamanism is truly a practice you can use for all sorts of situations.

How Does It Help?
Step 14
Application for Everyday Life

Connecting to the **natural world** brings you closer to the raising of consciousness that Shamanism promotes. Some suggestions:

1. When you see an animal, insect or bird come near you or share your space, ask if it has a message for you. Listen quietly and trust the message you receive. See if it resonates with you.
2. Take nature walks and notice the mystery of nature and how everything interacts. An example is: "Entelechy is a word Aristotle used to describe higher guidance and purpose. It is the entelechy of an acorn to be an oak, of a baby to be a grown up human being. It is being in the flow." Jean Houston
3. Keep a journal or notes on your phone when you get a message.
4. If the message requires you to do something, do it. Notice how you feel once you do.

How to Apply Shamanism to Modern Life

Working with your animal spirits is a relationship and all relationships need nurturing and attention. Here are some ways to do that:

- Honor your power animal by creating a special space for a picture, statue or wear a piece of jewelry of the animal spirit.
- Donate to a cause that supports animals in nature. Such organizations like: www.worldwildlife.com, www.africanwildlife.com,
- www.wcs.org.
- www.support.nature.org or www.greenpeace.org
- Volunteer to an organization.
- Help to take the stigma out of talking about Shamanism and share this book with your friends and others.
- Attend live and on-line events featuring Shamans such as www.theshiftnetwork.com or https://www.shamanlinks.net/shaman-info/resource-links/
- Join my meet-up: https://www.meetup.com/The-Ordinary-Shaman/

How Does It Help?
Step 15
Shamanism Seeks The Highest Good

When you open your mind to the gifts that practicing Shamanism gives you there is new hope for you and the whole world. When you journey to your guides and attune with nature you allow the unfolding of the infinite all around you. You get in touch with the wider universe. What does that mean for you?

1. As you step into the peripheral expanses around you, you are making the invisible visible to you.
2. Quieting your mind and listening to your power animal's messages enables you to hear what is meant for your highest good means they have the best intentions for you and your life.
3. By practicing ceremony, journeying, being in nature, sitting in quiet reflection, dancing to the tune of your true self and the practical aspects that your guides reveal to you, you can see, hear and sense messages that are good for all humankind.

The Meaning of the Highest Good

During a ritual, ceremony, group or individual journeying experience the goal is always for the highest good.

- That means what is best for all.
- As you expand your experience, you will begin to spread that highest good to more people, your friends, community, and beyond. You will make a difference.
- You may have trouble remembering who you really are; who you came here to be, what you want to accomplish.
- The practice of Shamanism makes those rumblings louder. Now is your time to listen.
- Remember, **you are never alone.** All you need to do is ask for help, guidance and the presence of your compassionate spirit guide.

If you have questions or want to explore Shamanism more, do not hesitate to contact me at chris@christinealisa.com and check out my website at www.ChristineAlisa.com for more information on Shamanism.

Thank you for reading this book. I hope it opened the curiosity in your mind and soul.

You've finished. Before you go…

Tweet/share that you finished this book.

Please star rate this book.

Reviews are solid gold to writers. Please take a few minutes to give us some itty bitty feedback.

ABOUT THE AUTHOR

Christine Alisa, MS is a shamanic practitioner, energy teacher, Licensed Marriage Family Therapist, a past life regression therapist and an international speaker and trainer.

She summons the inner soul to transformation while providing the platform, medium and composition for that experience. She peels back the layers of the unknown core issues revealing the open person inside who attracts new joyful experiences. Your internal voice opens to new possibilities when you leave her office.

Her workshops and trainings, have been described as "amazing to witness and experience how…access to the emotional brain…was unfolding throughout the session."

Christine leads an ongoing meet-up called The Ordinary Shaman where she teaches the principles of Shamanism and Journeying to new and seasoned practitioners. Check out her website where Christine offers a Complimentary Discovery Session.

She is the author of three books for parents, therapists and healers including: *Your Amazing Itty Bitty Communicating with Your Teenager Book: 15 Essential Steps to Improving Your Relationship with Your Teen.*

Contact her at:

chris@christinealisa.com
www.christinealisa.com
(562) 619-5883

If you enjoyed this book you might also like…

- **Your Amazing Itty Bitty® Self-Esteem Book** – Jade Elizabeth

- **Your Amazing Itty Bitty® Stress Reduction Book** – Denise Thomson

- **Your Amazing Itty Bitty® Heal Your Body Book** – Patricia Garza Pinto

Or many of the other Your Amazing Itty Bitty books available on line.

www.ingramcontent.com/pod-product-compliance
Lightning Source LLC
Chambersburg PA
CBHW061305040426
42444CB00010B/2526